THE JPS B'NAI MITZVAH TORAH COMMENTARY

Va-'era' (Exodus 6:2–9:35)
Haftarah (Ezekiel 28:25–29:21)

Rabbi Jeffrey K. Salkin

The Jewish Publication Society · Philadelphia
University of Nebraska Press · Lincoln

INTRODUCTION

News flash: the most important thing about becoming bar or bat mitzvah isn't the party. Nor is it the presents. Nor even being able to celebrate with your family and friends—as wonderful as those things are. Nor is it even standing before the congregation and reading the prayers of the liturgy—as important as that is.

No, the most important thing about becoming bar or bat mitzvah is sharing Torah with the congregation. And why is that? Because of all Jewish skills, that is the most important one.

Here is what is true about rites of passage: you can tell what a culture values by the tasks it asks its young people to perform on their way to maturity. In American culture, you become responsible for driving, responsible for voting, and yes, responsible for drinking responsibly.

In some cultures, the rite of passage toward maturity includes some kind of trial, or a test of strength. Sometimes, it is a kind of "outward bound" camping adventure. Among the Maasai tribe in Africa, it is traditional for a young person to hunt and kill a lion. In some Hispanic cultures, fifteen year-old girls celebrate the *quinceañera*, which marks their entrance into maturity.

What is Judaism's way of marking maturity? It combines both of these rites of passage: *responsibility* and *test*. You show that you are on your way to becoming a *responsible* Jewish adult through a public *test* of strength and knowledge—reading or chanting Torah, and then teaching it to the congregation.

This is the most important Jewish ritual mitzvah (commandment), and that is how you demonstrate that you are, truly, bar or bat mitzvah—old enough to be responsible for the mitzvot.

What Is Torah?

So, what exactly is the Torah? You probably know this already, but let's review.

The Torah (teaching) consists of "the five books of Moses," sometimes also called the *chumash* (from the Hebrew word *chameish,* which means "five"), or, sometimes, the Greek word Pentateuch (which means "the five teachings").

Here are the five books of the Torah, with their common names and their Hebrew names.

> **Genesis (The beginning), which in Hebrew is Bere'shit (from the first words—"When God began to create").** Bere'shit spans the years from Creation to Joseph's death in Egypt. Many of the Bible's best stories are in Genesis: the creation story itself; Adam and Eve in the Garden of Eden; Cain and Abel; Noah and the Flood; and the tales of the Patriarchs and Matriarchs, Abraham, Isaac, Jacob, Sarah, Rebekah, Rachel, and Leah. It also includes one of the greatest pieces of world literature, the story of Joseph, which is actually the oldest complete novel in history, comprising more than one-quarter of all Genesis.

> **Exodus (Getting out), which in Hebrew is Shemot (These are the names).** Exodus begins with the story of the Israelite slavery in Egypt. It then moves to the rise of Moses as a leader, and the Israelites' liberation from slavery. After the Israelites leave Egypt, they experience the miracle of the parting of the Sea of Reeds (or "Red Sea"); the giving of the Ten Commandments at Mount Sinai; the idolatry of the Golden Calf; and the design and construction of the Tabernacle and of the ark for the original tablets of the law, which our ancestors carried with them in the desert. Exodus also includes various ethical and civil laws, such as "You shall not wrong a stranger or oppress him, for you were strangers in the land of Egypt" (22:20).

> **Leviticus (about the Levites), or, in Hebrew, Va-yikra' (And God called).** It goes into great detail about the kinds of sacrifices that the ancient Israelites brought as offerings; the laws of ritual purity; the animals that were permitted and forbidden for eating (the beginnings of the tradition of kashrut, the Jewish dietary laws); the diagnosis of various skin diseases; the ethical laws of holiness; the ritual calendar of the Jewish year; and various agricultural laws concerning the treatment of the Land of Israel. Leviticus is basically the manual of ancient Judaism.

➤ Numbers (because the book begins with the census of the Israelites), or, in Hebrew, Be-midbar (In the wilderness). The book
describes the forty years of wandering in the wilderness and the
various rebellions against Moses. The constant theme: "Egypt
wasn't so bad. Maybe we should go back." The greatest rebellion
against Moses was the negative reports of the spies about the
Land of Israel, which discouraged the Israelites from wanting to
move forward into the land. For that reason, the "wilderness generation" must die off before a new generation can come into maturity and finish the journey.

➤ Deuteronomy (The repetition of the laws of the Torah), or, in
Hebrew, Devarim (The words). The final book of the Torah is,
essentially, Moses's farewell address to the Israelites as they pre-
pare to enter the Land of Israel. Here we find various laws that
had been previously taught, though sometimes with different
wording. Much of Deuteronomy contains laws that will be important to the Israelites as they enter the Land of Israel—laws
concerning the establishment of a monarchy and the ethics of
warfare. Perhaps the most famous passage from Deuteronomy
contains the *Shema,* the declaration of God's unity and unique-
ness, and the *Ve-ahavta,* which follows it. Deuteronomy ends with
the death of Moses on Mount Nebo as he looks across the Jordan
Valley into the land that he will not enter.

Jews read the Torah in sequence—starting with Bere'shit right after Simchat Torah in the autumn, and then finishing Devarim on the
following Simchat Torah. Each Torah portion is called a parashah (di-
vision; sometimes called a *sidrah,* a place in the order of the Torah
reading). The stories go around in a full circle, reminding us that we
can always gain more insights and more wisdom from the Torah. This
means that if you don't "get" the meaning this year, don't worry—it
will come around again.

And What Else? The Haftarah

We read or chant the Torah from the Torah scroll—the most sacred
thing that a Jewish community has in its possession. The Torah is

written without vowels, and the ability to read it and chant it is part of the challenge and the test.

But there is more to the synagogue reading. Every Torah reading has an accompanying haftarah reading. Haftarah means "conclusion," because there was once a time when the service actually ended with that reading. Some scholars believe that the reading of the haftarah originated at a time when non-Jewish authorities outlawed the reading of the Torah, and the Jews read the haftarah sections instead. In fact, in some synagogues, young people who become bar or bat mitzvah read very little Torah and instead read the entire haftarah portion.

The haftarah portion comes from the Nevi'im, the prophetic books, which are the second part of the Jewish Bible. It is either read or chanted from a Hebrew Bible, or maybe from a booklet or a photocopy.

The ancient sages chose the haftarah passages because their themes reminded them of the words or stories in the Torah text. Sometimes, they chose *haftarah* with special themes in honor of a festival or an upcoming festival.

Not all books in the prophetic section of the Hebrew Bible consist of prophecy. Several are historical. For example:

The book of Joshua tells the story of the conquest and settlement of Israel.

The book of Judges speaks of the period of early tribal rulers who would rise to power, usually for the purpose of uniting the tribes in war against their enemies. Some of these leaders are famous: Deborah, the great prophetess and military leader, and Samson, the biblical strong man.

The books of Samuel start with Samuel, the last judge, and then move to the creation of the Israelite monarchy under Saul and David (approximately 1000 BCE).

The books of Kings tell of the death of King David, the rise of King Solomon, and how the Israelite kingdom split into the Northern Kingdom of Israel and the Southern Kingdom of Judah (approximately 900 BCE).

And then there are the books of the prophets, those spokesmen for God whose words fired the Jewish conscience. Their names are immortal: Isaiah, Jeremiah, Ezekiel, Amos, Hosea, among others.

Someone once said: "There is no evidence of a biblical prophet ever being invited back a second time for dinner." Why? Because the prophets were tough. They had no patience for injustice, apathy, or hypocrisy. No one escaped their criticisms. Here's what they taught:

> God commands the Jews to behave decently toward one another. In fact, God cares more about basic ethics and decency than about ritual behavior.
> God chose the Jews *not* for special privileges, but for special duties to humanity.
> As bad as the Jews sometimes were, there was always the possibility that they would improve their behavior.
> As bad as things might be now, it will not always be that way. Someday, there will be universal justice and peace. Human history is moving forward toward an ultimate conclusion that some call the Messianic Age: a time of universal peace and prosperity for the Jewish people and for all the people of the world.

Your Mission—To Teach Torah to the Congregation

On the day when you become bar or bat mitzvah, you will be reading, or chanting, Torah—in Hebrew. You will be reading, or chanting, the haftarah—in Hebrew. That is the major skill that publicly marks the becoming of bar or bat mitzvah. But, perhaps even more important than that, you need to be able to teach something about the Torah portion, and perhaps the haftarah as well.

And that is where this book comes in. It will be a very valuable resource for you, and your family, in the b'nai mitzvah process.

Here is what you will find in it:

> A brief **summary** of every Torah portion. This is a basic overview of the portion; and, while it might not refer to everything in the Torah portion, it will explain its most important aspects.
> A list of the **major ideas** in the Torah portion. The purpose: to make the Torah portion real, in ways that we can relate to. Every Torah portion contains unique ideas, and when you put all

of those ideas together, you actually come up with a list of Judaism's most important ideas.

> Two ***divrei Torah*** ("words of Torah," or "sermonettes") for each portion. These *divrei Torah* explain significant aspects of the Torah portion in accessible, reader-friendly language. Each *devar Torah* contains references to **traditional** Jewish sources (those that were written before the modern era), as well as **modern** sources and quotes. We have searched, far and wide, to find sources that are unusual, interesting, and not just the "same old stuff" that many people already know about the Torah portion. Why did we include these minisermons in the volume? Not because we want you to simply copy those sermons and pass them off as your own (that would be cheating), though you are free to quote from them. We included them so that you can see what is possible—how you can try to make meaning for yourself out of the words of Torah.

> **Connections:** This is perhaps the most valuable part. It's a list of questions that you can ask yourself, or that others might help you think about—any of which can lead to the creation of your *devar Torah.*

Note: you don't have to like everything that's in a particular Torah portion. Some aren't that loveable. Some are hard to understand; some are about religious practices that people today might find confusing, and even offensive; some contain ideas that we might find totally outmoded.

But this doesn't have to get in the way. After all, most kids spend a lot of time thinking about stories that contain ideas that modern people would find totally bizarre. Any good medieval fantasy story falls into that category.

And we also believe that, if you spend just a little bit of time with those texts, you can begin to understand what the author was trying to say.

This volume goes one step further. Sometimes, the haftarah comes off as a second thought, and no one really thinks about it. We have tried to solve that problem by including a **summary** of each haftarah, and then a mini-sermon on the haftarah. This will help you learn how these sacred words are relevant to today's world, and even to your own life.

All Bible quotations come from the NJPS translation, which is found in the many different editions of the JPS TANAKH; in the Conservative movement's *Etz Hayim: Torah and Commentary;* in the Reform movement's *Torah: A Modern Commentary;* and in other Bible commentaries and study guides.

How Do I Write a *Devar Torah*?

It really is easier than it looks.

There are many ways of thinking about the *devar Torah*. It is, of course, a short sermon on the meaning of the Torah (and, perhaps, the haftarah) portion. It might even be helpful to think of the *devar Torah* as a "book report" on the portion itself.

The most important thing you can know about this sacred task is: *Learn* the words. *Love* the words. Teach people what it could mean to *live* the words.

Here's a basic outline for a *devar Torah:*

"My Torah portion is (name of portion) _____,
  from the book of _____, chapter

  _____.

"In my Torah portion, we learn that _____
  (Summary of portion)

"For me, the most important lesson of this Torah portion is (what
  is the best thing in the portion? Take the portion as a whole;
  your *devar Torah* does not have to be only, or specifically, on the
  verses that you are reading).

"As I learned my Torah portion, I found myself wondering:

  > *Raise a question that the Torah portion itself raises.*
  > *"Pick a fight"* with the portion. Argue with it.
  > *Answer a question* that is listed in the "Connections" section of
    each Torah portion.
  > *Suggest a question to your rabbi* that you would want the rabbi
    to answer in his or her own *devar Torah* or sermon.

"I have lived the values of the Torah by _____
(here, you can talk about how the Torah portion relates to your
own life. If you have done a mitzvah project, you can talk about
that here).

How To Keep It from Being Boring
(and You from Being Bored)

Some people just don't like giving traditional speeches. From our per-
spective, that's really okay. Perhaps you can teach Torah in a different
way—one that makes sense to you.

> Write an "open letter" to one of the characters in your Torah por-
> tion. "Dear Abraham: I hope that your trip to Canaan was not too
> hard . . ." "Dear Moses: Were you afraid when you got the Ten
> Commandments on Mount Sinai? I sure would have been . . ."
> Write a news story about what happens. Imagine yourself to
> be a television or news reporter. "Residents of neighboring cit-
> ies were horrified yesterday as the wicked cities of Sodom and
> Gomorrah were burned to the ground. Some say that God was
> responsible . . ."
> Write an imaginary interview with a character in your Torah portion.
> Tell the story from the point of view of another character, or a mi-
> nor character, in the story. For instance, tell the story of the Gar-
> den of Eden from the point of view of the serpent. Or the story
> of the Binding of Isaac from the point of view of the ram, which
> was substituted for Isaac as a sacrifice. Or perhaps the story of
> the sale of Joseph from the point of view of his coat, which was
> stripped off him and dipped in a goat's blood.
> Write a poem about your Torah portion.
> Write a song about your Torah portion.
> Write a play about your Torah portion, and have some friends act
> it out with you.
> Create a piece of artwork about your Torah portion.

The bottom line is: Make this a joyful experience. Yes—it could
even be fun.

The Very Last Thing You Need to Know at This Point

The Torah scroll is written without vowels. Why? Don't *sofrim* (Torah scribes) know the vowels?

Of course they do.

So, why do they leave the vowels out?

One reason is that the Torah came into existence at a time when sages were still arguing about the proper vowels, and the proper pronunciation.

But here is another reason: The Torah text, as we have it today, and as it sits in the scroll, is actually *an unfinished work*. Think of it: the words are just sitting there. Because they have no vowels, it is as if they have no voice.

When we read the Torah publicly, we give voice to the ancient words. And when we find meaning in those ancient words, and we talk about those meanings, those words jump to life. They enter our lives. They make our world deeper and better.

Mazal tov to you, and your family. This is your journey toward Jewish maturity. Love it.

THE TORAH

❖ Va-'era': Exodus 6:2–9:35

It was not as if Moses had no experience with the God of the Israelites. He had first met that God in the form of a burning bush. Now it was time for Moses to meet God again. The last time that Moses met God, God was "the God of your father the God of Abraham, the God of Isaac, and the God of Jacob" (3:6). This time, God has a "new" name—a name that is mysterious and unpronounceable.

God reassures Moses that God has noticed the suffering of the Israelites in Egypt, and that it will be Moses's job to appeal to Pharaoh to let them go. But Moses isn't so sure about that. He tries to get out of this job; he protests that he's got a speech impediment and doesn't talk very well. And so, Moses's brother, Aaron, becomes his spokesperson.

They approach Pharaoh and demand that the Israelites be freed—with a little help from some old-fashioned snake tricks. But Pharaoh isn't impressed; he doesn't get it. He needs a wake-up call. That's how the plagues started—turning the Nile into blood, bringing on frogs, swarms of insects, cattle disease, boils, and hail. Throughout it all, Pharaoh remains stubborn, and refuses to let the Israelites go.

Summary

> God reveals a new divine name to Moses—YHVH (*Yud Heh Vav Heh*), which Jews now pronounce as "Adonai." (6:2–13)

> Moses insists that he has trouble speaking, which will make it very difficult for him to lead the Israelites out of Egypt. (6:30)

> Moses and Aaron get into a war of magical powers with the magicians of Egypt to see who has the most power—the God of the Israelites, or the gods of the Egyptians. (7:8–18)

> God brings the first plagues upon the Egyptians. The Nile turns to blood; frogs appeared, lice, swarms of insects, cattle disease, boils, and hail. Throughout it all, Pharaoh's heart is "hardened," which means that he is unable to make the wise decision to let the Israelites go—though, at times, he gets pretty close to figuring that out. (7:19–9:34)

The Big Ideas

- **We can never know God entirely.** God reveals a new name to Moses—*Yud Heh Vav Heh*. But the name is mysterious, and perhaps even unpronounceable. In the ancient world, to know someone's name means to have some kind of power over that person, and you cannot have power over God.

- **Disability does not mean that you have to be helpless.** Even though Moses has trouble speaking, he's still able to be a leader of his people. Disabilities need not keep people from doing great and important things.

- **Only God is God.** The plagues were not just nasty acts that God performed against the Egyptians; they were acts aimed against the gods of Egypt. The whole purpose of the plagues was to give Pharaoh a lesson in God's power.

- **Everyone (except for Pharaoh) has free will.** God "froze" Pharaoh's ability to think for himself, so that he would not let the Israelites go. If he had in fact done so, then Pharaoh would have been the agent of freedom, not God.

Divrei Torah

GOD'S NEW NAME

A teenager (perhaps you) applies for a special summer program. The application asks: "name of father." The kid writes: "Dad."

It's a sweet and understandable error. But, in fact, "Dad" is not your father's name. Well, it is to you. His real name is (let's just say) Harold Schwartz. You call your father Dad, but his boss might call him Harold. The person who works at the bank might call him Mr. Schwartz. Your mother might call him Hal, or at times "honey," "dear," or other affectionate nicknames. His siblings might refer to him by his childhood nickname Hally. So, the truth is: your father has many names—simultaneously. You probably do as well.

In this Torah portion God tells Moses that the Patriarchs knew God as El Shaddai. A midrash says: "God said to Moses: Many times I appeared to Abraham, Isaac and Jacob as El Shaddai, but they never asked My name nor questioned My ways! Yet You ask my name?" In fact, there are many different names for God, and you already know some of them, like Elohim, Adonai—and on the High Holy Days, Avinu Malkheinu.

God's "new" name is YHVH, *Yud Heh Vav Heh*. For two thousand years, Jews have pronounced it Adonai—"my Lord," though some people simply translate this as "the Eternal."

All those "names" for God are just guesses. We don't know how to pronounce God's "real" name; maybe we never knew it. Once a year, on Yom Kippur, the High Priest would enter the Holy of Holies in the ancient Temple and say God's name. But, somehow, the vowels of God's name got lost—along with the real pronunciation of God's four-letter name. Is it pronounced "Yahweh"? Is it Jehovah (as in the Christian missionary group Jehovah's Witnesses)? We not only don't know how to say it; it is considered bad form to even try. That's why some Jews simply refer to God as *ha-Shem* (the Name).

YHVH seems to be related to the Hebrew verb root *heh-vav-heh*, which means "to be." YHVH could mean "that which causes to be," which would be a pretty good way to describe God.

The contemporary theologian Arthur Green believes that YHVH is a simultaneous rendition of the Hebrew root "to be" in its past, present, and perfect tenses: "As though it really was 'Is-Was-Will Be.' It is a verb caught in motion."

So, God's name is something like "iswaswillbe." It is impossible for us to say God's "real" name. As it is impossible to really know God's nature, although we strive to imitate God's ways. That's the problem and the challenge.

MOSES, SPEAK UP!

It's called being tongue tied. Some people call it stuttering. Others call it stammering. Whatever you want to call it, it's difficult and annoying. And yet, many people overcome speech impediments like this one, and they become great leaders.

Take Moses, for example. In fact, Moses has two kinds of speech problems. But they are very different, and they tell us a lot about who Moses really is.

One of these impediments has to do with the way that Moses actually speaks. Moses refers to himself as being *kaved peh* and *kaved lashon* (4:10), which is translated as "slow of speech and slow of tongue." Moses is either not an orator, or he has a speech defect. Just as Jacob was wounded and limps, Moses is also "wounded" and "limps" with his speech.

How did that happen? An ancient legend says that when Moses was an infant, Pharaoh placed before him a gold vessel and a live coal. If he reached for the gold, he would have proven himself to be a future threat. If he went for the coal—no problem. A midrash tells us, "The infant Moses was about to reach forth for the gold when the angel Gabriel came and moved his hand so that it seized the coal, and he thrust his hand with the live coal into his mouth, so that his tongue was burnt, with the result that he became slow of speech and of tongue."

So maybe that is how Moses developed his speech defect. More likely, he was simply born with a problem or failed to develop typical language skills. But the Torah also says that Moses is *aral sefatayim* (6:12). While most translations say that this means "impeded speech," it really means that he has "uncircumcised lips" (or "uncircumcised language").

Uncircumcised *lips?* What? When the Bible says that someone is uncircumcised, it may not mean physical circumcision. To be *arel* or *aral,* "uncircumcised," can also mean that someone is a foreigner. Moses was not really an Israelite. Having grown up in the royal court, Moses would have seemed foreign to the Israelites. They would not have accepted him as their leader. Perhaps Moses is saying that he doesn't know Hebrew because he has been so cut off from his people. That also would have created a problem in communication.

Another interpretation—this one from a Hasidic sage, Yehudah Aryeh Leib of Ger. "As long as there are those who will listen, then there can be those who speak, because the power of the leader issues from the people. For this reason, if the children of Israel listen to Moses, his mouth would be opened, his speech would be fluent, and his words would reach Pharaoh. But if they don't want to listen to him he would be made into one of impeded speech." Moses has a hard time not only getting Pharaoh to listen, but also his very own people to listen.

How often we see this happening! It's not enough for the leader to be able to speak, to be eloquent and forceful. People have to listen. Sometimes that's the hardest part of all.

Connections

> Can you think of examples of people who had disabilities or physical challenges and were still able to do great things? What do you think made them successful at what they did?

> Have you ever been a leader, or tried to lead? What have been some of your challenges in doing so?

> Were there any times when you had difficulty being understood, or understanding someone else? What was that like? How did you overcome it?

> Another interpretation of God's Name, yhvh, is that each Hebrew character is "open —*yud* on the left-hand side, *heh* on the bottom (there is a space between the two prongs of the letter), and *vav* on all sides. What are you open to learning, experiencing, and doing?

THE HAFTARAH

❖ Va'era': Ezekiel 28:25–29:21

Some people say that the prophet Ezekiel was, well, crazy. He had all sorts of wild visions, including imagining that God was traveling across the heavens in a chariot. But one thing is for sure: he really understood the international situation in the world he lived in. Ezekiel was a prophet who started making prophecies in the final days of the kingdom of Judah, and who went with the Judeans into exile in Babylonia. The people of Judah hoped that if they made an alliance with Egypt they would avoid destruction at the hands of the Babylonians.

Ezekiel knew that this was the wrong decision. He knew that Egypt was an untrustworthy ally, and that it would itself be destroyed. So, he engaged in a loud, bitter rant against the Egyptians. But here's the interesting part: when Ezekiel was screaming about the Egyptian problem of his own day, he was thinking about another earlier Egyptian problem— the arrogance of the ancient Pharaoh in the time of the Exodus from Egypt. So, we can read this haftarah not only as a criticism of the Egypt of Ezekiel's time, but also a criticism of the Egypt of the time of Moses.

Jerk Alert

Yes, I know "jerk" is a strong word, and I do not take name-calling lightly. But do you know any jerks? You probably do. And what, exactly, is a jerk? The Merriam-Webster Dictionary defines "jerk" as "a stupid person or a person who is not well-liked or who treats other people badly."

If you read the Bible, here is what you will discover: the overwhelming majority of non-Israelite kings are jerks. (And, to be fair, there are also a few kings of Israel who fit that description). King Nebuchadnezzar of Babylon, who destroyed the ancient kingdom of Judah during Ezekiel's time, certainly treated people badly. In the Bible he was not well liked and is portrayed as not only evil, but, despite his power, also as a helpless, pitiful, broken man.

Then there's King Ahasuerus, in the book of Esther and a famous character in the Purim story. He is hardly the brightest candle in the menorah. In fact, the Rabbinic tradition refers to him as *ha-melekh ha-tipeish,* "the foolish king." He is something of a buffoon and party animal who fortunately has the good sense to listen to Esther.

But, the winner of the Greatest Biblical Jerk Contest is none other than Pharaoh, king of Egypt. The Pharaoh portrayed in the Torah portion is a guy who simply cannot get it right. Somewhere in the back of his mind, he knows that he should be letting the ancient Israelites go, but he simply cannot do so. God has hardened his heart, and then he hardens his own heart—which does not mean an overdose of cholesterol, but implies a stubbornness so severe that he is actually unable to do what is right. That's why God has to bring the plagues on Egypt.

It turns out that "jerkitude" ran in the Pharaoh family. Centuries later, the prophet Ezekiel yells at the Israelites: Don't put any trust in Egypt! And then, to make it even better, Ezekiel turns his attention on the Pharaoh of his time and disses him, big time. "In the tenth year, on the twelfth day of the tenth month, the word of the Lord came to me: O mortal, turn your face against Pharaoh king of Egypt, and prophesy against him and against all Egypt. Speak these words: Thus said the Lord God: I am going to deal with you, O Pharaoh king of Egypt, mighty monster, sprawling in your channels, who said, My Nile is my own; I made it for myself" (29:1–3).

In particular, what disturbs Ezekiel about this Pharaoh? (You might rightly ask at this point: have we ever met a Pharaoh that we've liked?) Ezekiel compares Pharaoh to a crocodile, a reptilian creature that prowls the Nile. That is bad enough, but what else does Ezekiel say about this Pharaoh?

When Pharaoh said, "My Nile is my own; I made it for myself," he is saying that he is a god—and that he created the Nile—for himself! Like the original Pharaoh this ruler is clueless. The guy simply doesn't understand the words of Proverbs: "Pride goes before ruin; arrogance, before failure" (Prov. 16:18).

But even more than that: you can read the Hebrew version of Pharaoh's boast, "I made it [the Nile] for myself," as meaning "I made myself." When you think that you are so great, so powerful, so successful, that you have made yourself—you are so full of yourself, so arrogant, that you will care nothing for others. As Rabbi Andrea Carol Steinberger teaches: "It is as if the haftarah is warning Pharaoh: 'Do not see yourself as the definer of life, of what is possible and impossible to do.'"

Ezekiel compares Pharaoh to a monster, and that's bad enough. But Ezekiel's audience would have known that in the story of creation, God created the great sea monsters; they didn't create themselves. If only the Pharaohs of history knew that, that nobody is God and nobody creates themselves. A little humility can go a long way.

❖ Notes

CPSIA information can be obtained
at www.ICGtesting.com
Printed in the USA
LVHW08s0951050818
585984LV00004B/436/P

9 780827 613720